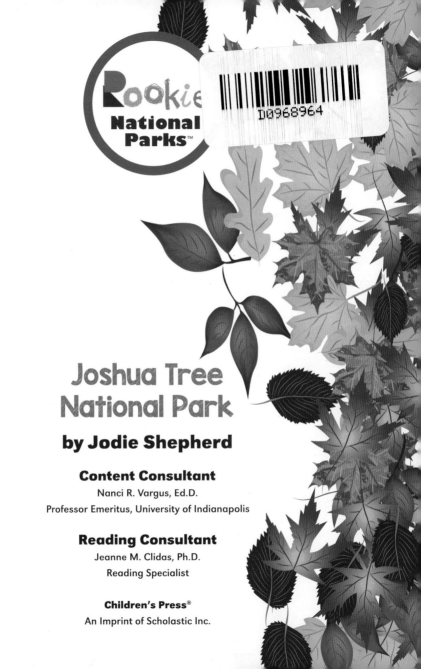

Rookie National Parks™

Joshua Tree National Park

by Jodie Shepherd

Content Consultant

Nanci R. Vargus, Ed.D.
Professor Emeritus, University of Indianapolis

Reading Consultant

Jeanne M. Clidas, Ph.D.
Reading Specialist

Children's Press®
An Imprint of Scholastic Inc.

D0968964

Library of Congress Cataloging-in-Publication Data

Names: Shepherd, Jodie, author.
Title: Joshua Tree National Park/by Jodie Shepherd.
Description: New York, NY: Children's Press, an Imprint of Scholastic Inc., 2018.
Series: Rookie national parks | Includes bibliographical references and index.
Identifiers: LCCN 2017058825| ISBN 9780531126509 (library binding) |
ISBN 9780531189016 (pbk.)
Subjects: LCSH: Joshua Tree National Park (Calif.)—Juvenile literature.
Classification: LCC F868.J6 S54 2018 | DDC 979.4/97—dc23
LC record available at https://lccn.loc.gov/2017058825

Produced by Spooky Cheetah Press
Design: Ed LoPresti Graphic Design
Creative Direction: Judith E. Christ for Scholastic Inc.

Published in 2019 by Children's Press, an imprint of Scholastic Inc.

Printed in Heshan, China 62

SCHOLASTIC, CHILDREN'S PRESS, ROOKIE NATIONAL PARKS™, and
associated logos are trademarks and/or registered trademarks of Scholastic Inc.

2 3 4 5 6 7 8 9 10 R 28 27 26 25 24 23 22 21 20 19

Scholastic, Inc., 557 Broadway, New York, NY 10012.

Photos ©: cover: KiskaMedia/iStockphoto; back cover background: CSP_billperry/age fotostock;
back cover inset: Stefan Eisend/LOOK-foto/Getty Images; cartoon fox throughout: Bill Mayer;
1-2: Cleo Design/Shutterstock; 3: Sierralara/iStockphoto; 4-5: LucynaKoch/iStockphoto;
6-7: Danita Delimont/Alamy Images; 8-9 background: Purestock/Thinkstock; 8 inset:
HanaBilikova/iStockphoto; 10-11 background: Andrew Peacock/Getty Images; 10 inset:
NPS/Alison Taggart-Barone/Flickr; 12-13: Visuals Unlimited, Inc./Patrick Smith/Getty Images;
14 top: Hulton Archive/Getty Images; 15: Pancaketom/Dreamstime; 16: Ted Soqui/Getty
Images; 17: Dr. Ken Wagner/Visuals Unlimited; 18-19: Sierralara/Getty Images; 18 inset:
Robert J. Erwin/Science Source; 20-21 background: Konrad Wothe/Minden Pictures;
21 inset: Michael Durham/Minden Pictures; 22-23 background: NaturePL/Superstock, Inc.;
23 top inset: Wayne Lynch/age fotostock; 23 bottom inset: Daniel Meissner/Getty Images;
24-25 background: David H. Carriere/Getty Images; 25 inset: Don Mason/Getty Images;
26 left: Paul Tessier/Shutterstock; 26 top center: Dorling Kindersley Universal Images Group/
Newscom; 26 bottom center: Martha Marks/Shutterstock; 26 top right: adogslifephoto/
iStockphoto; 26 bottom right: Jorn Vangoidtsenhoven/Dreamstime; 27 top left: Matt Jeppson/
Shutterstock; 27 bottom left: Ingrid Curry/Shutterstock; 27 top center: Takahashi Photography/
Shutterstock; 27 bottom center: P_Wei/iStockphoto; 27 top right: GlobalP/iStockphoto;
30 top left: NPS/Hannah Schwalbe/Flickr; 30 bottom left: Ovidiu Hrubaru/Shutterstock;
30 top right: George Ostertag/Alamy Images; 30 bottom right: B Christopher/Alamy Images;
31 center bottom: America/Alamy Images; 31 top: Wayne Lynch/age fotostock;
31 center top: NaturePL/Superstock, Inc.; 31 bottom: Michael Durham/Minden Pictures;
32: Robert Harding Picture Library.

Maps by Jim McMahon/Mapman.

Table of Contents

I am Ranger Red Fox, your tour guide. Are you ready for an amazing adventure in Joshua Tree?

Welcome to Joshua Tree National Park!

Joshua Tree is in Southern California. It was made a **national park** in 1994. People visit national parks to explore nature.

The park's name comes from the strange, spiky Joshua trees that grow there.

Joshua Tree National Park is the meeting place of two deserts, the Colorado Desert and the higher and cooler Mojave (moh-**hah**-vee) Desert. Different plants and animals live in each area.

Long ago, Native Americans lived here. They carved pictures and symbols into the rocks. Later, ranchers and gold and silver miners made the area their home.

Joshua Tree is one of our newer national parks.

United States

←California

Joshua Tree
National Park

N
W E
S

Pictures carved into rocks are called petroglyphs (**peh**-truh-gliffs).

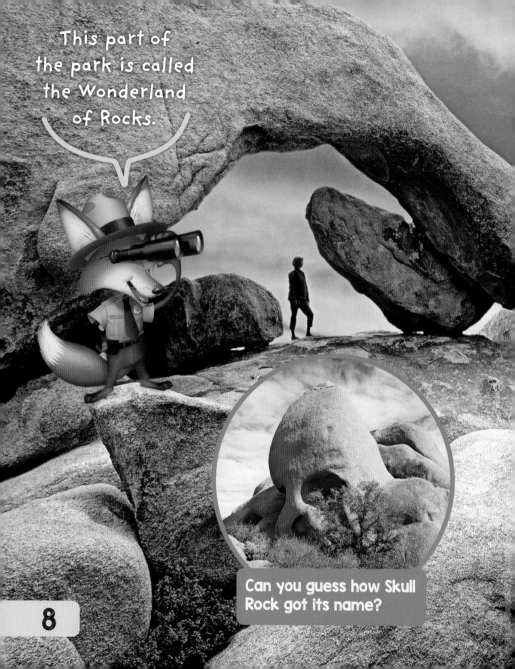

This part of the park is called the Wonderland of Rocks.

Can you guess how Skull Rock got its name?

8

Chapter 1

A Weird, Rocky World

Joshua Tree is known for its giant, strange-shaped boulders. The unusual shapes were formed when ice and strong rains and wind wore away parts of the rocks. Scientists believe that the oldest rocks in the park are about 1.7 billion years old.

This hiker climbed 1.5 miles (2 kilometers) to the top of Ryan Mountain.

There are many mountains in the park. The tallest is Quail Mountain, but only the most experienced hikers can get to the top. There are no developed trails on Quail. Visitors *can* trek to the top of Ryan Mountain, though. Ryan is the second-tallest mountain in the park.

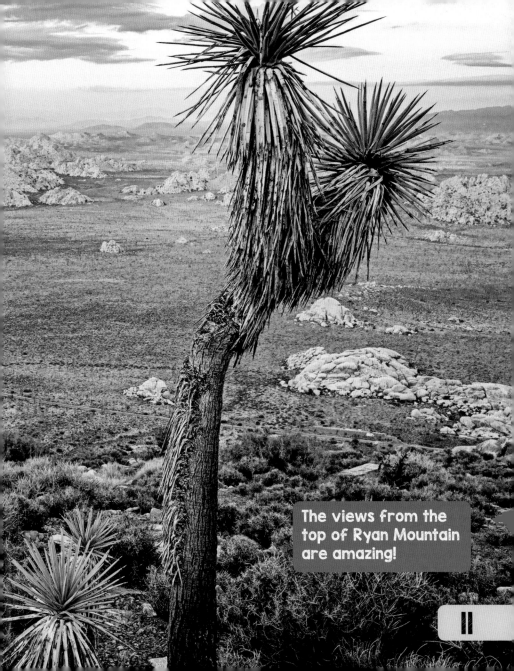

The views from the top of Ryan Mountain are amazing!

The park's animals and plants all need water to live.

There are five oases in the park.

Chapter 2

Water in the Desert?

Joshua Tree does not get a lot of rain. So every drop is important!

Two sources of water in the park are oases and springs. An oasis is a small green area where water can be found. Springs of water bubble up from underground streams.

Oases and springs made it possible for Native Americans to live in the area long ago. Ranchers who came later

Miners sifted through rocks, looking for gold.

needed the water for their cattle. The miners who arrived in the 1800s used the springs for drinking water, and to wash the gold they found.

There are nearly 300 abandoned gold and silver mines in the park.

This stamp mill was used to crush rocks. Miners looked for gold and silver in the rock dust.

Native Americans used the leaves of the Joshua tree to make baskets and shoes.

When Joshua trees are in bloom, they have white flowers.

16

Chapter 3

The Park's Trees and Plants

The Mojave Desert is the only place on Earth where the Joshua tree grows. Even though it looks like a cactus, it is not one. It is not a tree either! It's a type of yucca plant. The park's Black Rock Canyon is also home to piñon, juniper, and oak trees.

The yucca moth lays its eggs on the Joshua tree.

The creosote bush's odor has earned it the nickname "little stinker."

More than 750 kinds of plants grow in the park. They are all very good at surviving in the dry desert. Cacti can store water for a long time.

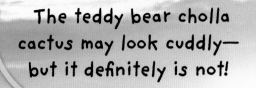

The teddy bear cholla cactus may look cuddly—but it definitely is not!

Teddy bear cholla (**cho**-ya) cacti grow in the park's cholla garden.

Desert flowers only bloom after the winter rains. If rains don't come, they save their water and wait until the next year to flower.

Joshua Tree's roadrunners can't fly far, but they can run fast!

Chapter 4

At Home in the Heat

It is not easy for animals to live in the desert. Most mammals in the park are small **rodents**. They hide underground or among rocks to escape the heat of the day. They are active at night, when it is cooler.

Kangaroo rats don't need to drink. They use water stored in the seeds they eat.

Reptiles are well **adapted** to desert life, too. They get the water they need from the food they eat. Many lizards and snakes never drink!

Seven different kinds of rattlesnakes live in Joshua Tree.

Thousands of different kinds of insects and spiders also live in the park. The honeypot ant stores so much food in its **abdomen** that it is hard for the ant to move!

The honeypot ant is shaped like a honey jar.

The chuckwalla lizard puffs out its chest when it is scared.

Joshua Tree National Park is an awe-inspiring place to visit. Whether you are hiking, climbing over boulders, or looking up at the night sky, you are sure to see something you have never seen before!

Visitors to the park can see millions of stars at night!

Joshua Tree has more than 8,000 climbing routes.

Imagine you could visit Joshua Tree National Park. What would you do there?

Here are some of the amazing animals that live in Joshua Tree National Park.

western pygmy
blue butterfly

desert scorpion

desert
bighorn sheep

Gambel's
quail

desert
kit fox

Wildlife by the Numbers
The park is home to about...

250 types of birds   **52** types of mammals

The desert tortoise is the largest reptile in the park.

red-spotted toad

Costa's hummingbird

desert black-tailed jackrabbit

Mojave desert tortoise

California mountain lion

46 types of reptiles and amphibians

0 native fish species

Where Is Ranger Red Fox?

Oh no! Ranger Red Fox has lost his way in the park. But you can help. Use the map and the clues below to find him.

1. Red Fox started at the Wonderland of Rocks, scrambling over and under the boulders.

2. Then he hiked southeast to Skull Rock. Ooh, kind of creepy!

3. He continued south and west to try his luck at Lost Horse Mine. He didn't find any gold.

4. Finally, he went east and discovered a huge cactus garden.

Help! Can you find me?

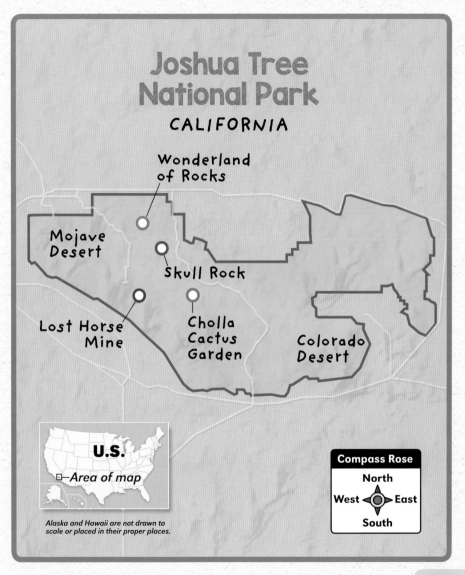

Joshua Tree National Park

CALIFORNIA

Wonderland of Rocks

Mojave Desert

Skull Rock

Lost Horse Mine

Cholla Cactus Garden

Colorado Desert

U.S.

□—Area of map

Alaska and Hawaii are not drawn to scale or placed in their proper places.

Compass Rose

North

West

East

South

Wildflower Tracker

Match each Joshua Tree wildflower to its name. Read the clues to help you.

A.

I. Chia
Clue: This spiky pink flower grows on a long stalk.

2. Notch-leaved phacelia
Clue: These small purple flowers are also called scorpionweed.

C.

B.

3. Desert mariposa lily
Clue: The name of this orange flower comes from the Spanish word for butterfly.

4. Desert dandelion
Clue: This pretty yellow flower with a red center closes its blooms at night.

D.

30

Answers: 1. D; 2. C; 3. A; 4. B

Glossary

abdomen (**ab**-duh-muhn): rear section of an insect's three-part body

adapted (uh-**dap**-ted): developed in a way to survive in a specific environment

national park (**nash**-uh-nuhl pahrk): area where the land and its animals are protected by the U.S. government

rodents (**roh**-duhnts): small mammals with sharp front teeth for gnawing

Index

Facts for Now

Visit this Scholastic Web site for more information on Joshua Tree National Park:
www.factsfornow.scholastic.com
Enter the keywords **Joshua Tree**

About the Author

Jodie Shepherd, who also writes under her real name, Leslie Kimmelman, is the award-winning author of dozens of fiction and nonfiction titles for children. She is also a children's book editor. She loves the funky-looking landscape of Joshua Tree National Park.